Poems of Love and Life for
LIBRA

Poems of Love and Life for
LIBRA
(23 SEPTEMBER to 23 OCTOBER)

JULIA & DEREK PARKER

Every effort has been made to acknowledge and contact the copyright holders for permission to reproduce material contained in this book. Any copyright holders who have been inadvertently omitted from acknowledgements and credits should contact the publisher and omissions will be rectified in subsequent editions.

An Ebury Press book
Published by Random House Australia Pty Ltd
Level 3, 100 Pacific Highway, North Sydney NSW 2060
www.randomhouse.com.au

First published by Ebury Press in 2013

Copyright © Julia & Derek Parker 2013

The moral right of the authors has been asserted.

All rights reserved. No part of this book may be reproduced or transmitted by any person or entity, including internet search engines or retailers, in any form or by any means, electronic or mechanical, including photocopying (except under the statutory exceptions provisions of the Australian *Copyright Act 1968*), recording, scanning or by any information storage and retrieval system without the prior written permission of Random House Australia.

Addresses for companies within the Random House Group can be found at
www.randomhouse.com.au/offices

National Library of Australia
Cataloguing-in-Publication entry

Parker, Julia, 1932–
Poems for love and life for Libra/Julia and Derek Parker.

ISBN 978 1 74275 787 2 (pbk.)

Libra (Astrology) – Poetry
Love poetry

Other Authors/Contributors:
Parker, Derek, 1932–

133.5272

Cover illustration by Rhian Nest James
Cover design by Cathie Glassby
Internal design and typesetting by Midland Typesetters, Australia
Printed in Australia by Griffin Press, an accredited ISO AS/NZS 14001:2004 Environmental Management System printer

Random House Australia uses papers that are natural, renewable and recyclable products and made from wood grown in sustainable forests. The logging and manufacturing processes are expected to conform to the environmental regulations of the country of origin.

TO ALL LOVERS OF POETRY AND ASTROLOGY

Introduction

In this book we have collected together poems which we believe will appeal to readers born between 23 September and 23 October, and therefore think of themselves as 'Librans' and read the paragraphs printed under *Libra* in newspaper and magazine astrology columns.

These are based on the idea of 'Sun-sign' or 'Star-sign' astrology – a very recent one, invented in the 1930s by an astrological journalist who wanted to simplify the extremely complex system used by professional astrologers over at least two thousand years of history. Though this may seem a simple idea, it is true that you and other people born when the Sun is 'in' Libra – that is, stands between the Earth and a particular background of sky – do share certain characteristics: for instance, Librans have an above-average need to be in a close personal relationship – so poems of love in all its phases are strongly represented.

Byron (p.3), Marlowe (p.10), Donne (p.12) and Elizabeth Barrett Browning (p.2) set the tone for this anthology. *Estrangement* (p.46), *The Lonely Maid* (p.50) and *When We Two Parted* (p.3) show other aspects of the effect of love on the susceptible Libra. Librans are also procrastinators – often indecisive and laid-back: *The Languid Lady* (p.108) is a believable portrait. They can reveal a decidedly racy, sensual side, which John Clare notes in *I Dreamt Of Robin* (p.8). Thomas Lodge (p.36) and Shelley (p.73) represent the Libran love of music, while W. S. Gilbert's typically acerbic view of ageing (p.88) will encourage Librans to never give up the fight to stay youthful in spirit and appearance. Incidentally, Longfellow may be a good poet, but he is an indifferent astrologer, for he mentions Scorpio (p.113) – but the Sun doesn't enter that sign until towards the end of October!

These poems are chosen because they reflect your attitude to life, your character and your interests, and also because they are associated with seasons, countries, and towns which are (in astrological terms) 'ruled' by the sign of Libra. The chances are that you will identify with many of their themes. Some we have chosen simply because we believe you will enjoy them, and that they will awaken or re-awaken your love of poetry.

J. P. & D. P.
Sydney, 2012.

Who Is It Comes?

Who is it comes hither through the dew
With measured steps? What maiden fair
   Walking across the breezy down,
    With eyes of deepest violet hue,
Full of deep knowledge, and with hair
   Of softest golden brown?
So starry-fair, so graceful tall –
Whose lucid eyelids when they fall,
   Are like the cloud that holds moonlight –
With such soft-rounded temples, like
White Venus whiter than all stars –
Whose coming ere she comes doth strike
On expectation, like the glow
Of the unrisen moon below
Dark firs, when creeping winds by night
Lay the long mist in streaks and bars.

– Alfred, Lord Tennyson

How Do I Love Thee?

How do I love thee? Let me count the ways.
I love thee to the depth and breadth and height
My soul can reach, when feeling out of sight
For the ends of Being and ideal Grace.
I love thee to the level of every day's
Most quiet need, by sun and candle-light.
I love thee freely, as men strive for Right;
I love thee purely, as they turn from Praise.
I love thee with the passion put to use
In my old griefs, and with my childhood's faith.
I love thee with a love I seemed to lose
With my lost saints, – I love thee with the breath,
Smiles, tears, of all my life! – and, if God choose,
I shall but love thee better after death.

– Elizabeth Barrett Browning

When We Two Parted

When we two parted
 In silence and tears,
Half broken-hearted
 To sever for years,
Pale grew thy cheek and cold,
 Colder thy kiss;
Truly that hour foretold
 Sorrow to this.

The dew of the morning
 Sunk chill on my brow –
It felt like the warning
 Of what I feel now.
Thy vows are all broken,
 And light is thy fame:
I hear thy name spoken,
 And share in its shame.

They name thee before me,
    A knell to mine ear;
A shudder comes o'er me –
    Why wert thou so dear?
They know not I knew thee,
    Who knew thee too well: –
Long, long shall I rue thee,
    Too deeply to tell.

In secret we met –
    In silence I grieve,
That thy heart could forget,
    Thy spirit deceive.
If I should meet thee
    After long years,
How should I greet thee? –
    With silence and tears

– Lord Byron

It Lies Not In Our Power To Love Or Hate

It lies not in our power to love or hate,
For will in us is overruled by fate.
When two are stripped, long ere the course begin,
We wish that one should love, the other win;
And one especially do we affect
Of two gold ingots, like in each respect:
The reason no man knows; let it suffice
What we behold is censured by our eyes.
Where both deliberate, the love is slight:
Who ever loved, that loved not at first sight?

– Christopher Marlowe

A Last Confession

What lively lad most pleasured me
Of all that with me lay?
I answer that I gave my soul
And loved in misery,
But had great pleasure with a lad
That I loved bodily.

Flinging from his arms I laughed
To think his passion such
He fancied that I gave a soul
Did but our bodies touch,
And laughed upon his breast to think
Beast gave beast as much.

I gave what other women gave
That stepped out of their clothes.
But when this soul, its body off,
Naked to naked goes,
He it has found shall find therein
What none other knows,

And give his own and take his own
And rule in his own right;
And though it loved in misery
Close and cling so tight,
There's not a bird of day that dare
Extinguish that delight.

– W. B. Yeats

I Dreamt Of Robin

I opened the casement this morn at starlight,
And, the moment I got out of bed,
The daisies were quaking about in their white
And the cowslip was nodding its head.
The grass was all shivers, the stars were all bright,
And Robin that should come at e'en –
I thought that I saw him, a ghost by moonlight,
Like a stalking horse stand on the green.

I went bed again and did nothing but dream
Of Robin and moonlight and flowers.
He stood like a shadow transfixed by a stream,
And I couldn't forget him for hours.
I'd just dropt asleep when I dreamed Robin spoke,
And the casement it gave such a shake,
As if every pane in the window was broke;
Such a patter the gravel did make.

So I up in the morning before the cock crew
And to strike me a light I sat down.
I saw from the door all his track in the dew
And, I guess, called 'Come in and sit down.'
And one, sure enough, tramples up to the door,
And who but young Robin his sen?[1]
And ere the old folks were half willing to stir
We met, kissed, and parted again.

– *John Clare*

---

1 sen – himself

The Passionate Shepherd To His Love

Come live with me and be my love,
And we will all the pleasures prove
That valleys, groves, hills, and fields,
Woods or steepy mountain yields.

And we will sit upon the rocks,
Seeing the shepherds feed their flocks,
By shallow rivers to whose falls
Melodious birds sing madrigals.

And I will make thee beds of roses
And a thousand fragrant posies,
A cap of flowers, and a kirtle
Embroidered all with leaves of myrtle;

A gown made of the finest wool
Which from our pretty lambs we pull;
Fair lined slippers for the cold,
With buckles of the purest gold;

A belt of straw and ivy buds,
With coral clasps and amber studs:
And if these pleasures may thee move,
Come live with me and be my love.

The shepherds' swains shall dance and sing
For thy delight each May morning:
If these delights thy mind may move,
Then live with me and be my love.

– Christopher Marlowe

The Bait

Come live with me, and be my love,
And we will some new pleasures prove
Of golden sands, and crystal brooks,
With silken lines, and silver hooks.

There will the river whispering run
Warmed by thy eyes, more than the sun;
And there the enamoured fish will stay,
Begging themselves they may betray.

When thou wilt swim in that live bath,
Each fish, which every channel hath,
Will amorously to thee swim,
Gladder to catch thee, than thou him.

If thou, to be so seen, be'st loth,
By sun or moon, thou darkenest both,
And if myself have leave to see,
I need not their light having thee.

Let others freeze with angling reeds,
And cut their legs with shells and weeds,
Or treacherously poor fish beset,
With strangling snare, or windowy net.

Let coarse bold hands from slimy nest
The bedded fish in banks out-wrest;
Or curious traitors, sleeve-silk flies,
Bewitch poor fishes' wandering eyes.

For thee, thou need'st no such deceit,
For thou thyself art thine own bait:
That fish, that is not catched thereby,
Alas, is wiser far than I.

– John Donne

Bobby Shafto

Bobby Shafto's gone to sea,
Silver buckles at his knee;
He'll come back and marry me,
Bonny Bobby Shafto!

Bobby Shafto's bright and fair,
Combing down his yellow hair;
He's my ain for evermair,
Bonny Bobby Shafto.

Bobby Shafto's getten a bairn,
For to dangle on his arm –
On his arm and on his knee;
Bobby Shafto loves me.

– *Anon*

Cupid Laid By His Brand, And Fell Asleep

Cupid laid by his brand, and fell asleep:
A maid of Dian's this advantage found,
And his love-kindling fire did quickly steep
In a cold valley-fountain of that ground;
Which borrowed from this holy fire of Love
A dateless lively heat, still to endure,
And grew a seething bath, which yet men prove
Against strange maladies a sovereign cure.
But at my mistress' eye Love's brand new-fired,
The boy for trial needs would touch my breast;
I, sick withal, the help of bath desired,
And thither hied, a sad distempered guest,
    But found no cure: the bath for my help lies
    Where Cupid got new fire – my mistress' eyes.

— *William Shakespeare*

A Spanish Love Song

From Andalusian gardens
I bring the rose and rue,
And leaves of subtle odour,
To weave a gift for you.
You'll know the reason wherefore
The sad is with the sweet;
My flowers may lie, as I would,
A carpet for your feet!
The heart – the heart is constant;
It holds its secret, Dear!
But often in the night time
I keep awake for fear.
I have no hope to whisper,
I have no prayer to send,
God save you from such passion!
God help you from such end!

You first, you last, you false love!
In dreams your lips I kiss,
And thus I greet your Shadow,
'Take this, and this, and this!'

When dews are on the casement,
And winds are in the pine,
I have you close beside me –
In sleep your mouth is mine.

I never see you elsewhere;
You never think of me;
But fired with fever for you
Content I am to be.
You will not turn, my Darling,
Nor answer when I call;
But yours are soul are body
And love of mine and all!

You splendid Spaniard! Listen –
My passion leaps to flame
For neck and cheek and dimple,
And cunning shades of shame!
I tell you, I would gladly
Give Hell myself to keep,
To cling to, half a moment,
The lips I taste in sleep.

– *Henry Kendall*

Ad Manus Puellæ[1]

I was always a lover of ladies' hands!
    Or ever mine heart came here to tryst,
For the sake of your carved white hands' commands;
    The tapering fingers, the dainty wrist;
    The hands of a girl were what I kissed.

I remember a hand like a *fleur-de-lys*[2]
    When it slid from its silken sheath, her glove;
With its odours passing ambergris:
    And that was the empty husk of a love.
    Oh, how shall I kiss your hands enough?

They are pale with the pallor of ivories;
    But they blush to the tips like a curled sea-shell:
What treasure, in kingly treasuries,
    Of gold, and spice for the thurible,
    Is sweet as her hands to hoard and tell!

---

1 *ad manus puellæ* – the girl's hand
2 fleur-de-lys – a stylised lily

I know not the way from your finger-tips,
    Nor how I shall gain the higher lands,
The citadel of your sacred lips:
    I am captive still of my pleasant bands,
    The hands of a girl, and most your hands.

– Ernest Dowson

The Measure Of Beauty

Give beauty all her right,
She's not to one form tied;
Each shape yields fair delight,
Where her perfections bide:
Helen, I grant, might pleasing be,
And Rosamond was as sweet as she.

Some the quick eye commends,
Some swelling lips and red;
Pale looks have many friends,
Through sacred sweetness bred:
Meadows have flowers that pleasure move,
Though roses are the flowers of love.

Free beauty is not bound
To one unmoved clime;
She visits every ground
And favours every time.
Let the old loves with mine compare,
My sovereign is as sweet as fair.

– *Thomas Campion*

Beauty And Beauty

When Beauty and Beauty meet
    All naked, fair to fair,
The earth is crying-sweet,
    And scattering-bright the air,
Eddying, dizzying, closing round,
    With soft and drunken laughter;
Veiling all that may befall
    After – after –

Where Beauty and Beauty met,
    Earth's still a-tremble there,
And winds are scented yet,
    And memory-soft the air,
Bosoming, folding glints of light,
    And shreds of shadowy laughter;
Not the tears that fill the years
    After – after –

– *Rupert Brooke*

Love's Philosophy

The fountains mingle with the river,
And the rivers with the ocean;
The winds of heaven mix forever
With a sweet emotion;
Nothing in the world is single;
All things by a law divine
In another's being mingle –
Why not I with thine?

See, the mountains kiss high heaven,
And the waves clasp one another;
No sister flower could be forgiven
If it disdained its brother;
And the sunlight clasps the earth,
And the moonbeams kiss the sea; –
What are all these kissings worth,
If thou kiss not me?

– *Percy Bysshe Shelley*

Echo

Come to me in the silence of the night;
Come in the speaking silence of a dream;
Come with soft rounded cheeks and eyes as bright
As sunlight on a stream;
Come back in tears,
O memory, hope, love of finished years.

Oh dream how sweet, too sweet, too bitter-sweet,
Whose wakening should have been in Paradise,
Where souls brim-full of love abide and meet;
Where thirsting longing eyes
Watch the slow door
That opening, letting in, lets out no more.

Yet come to me in dreams, that I may live
My very life again though cold in death:
Come back to me in dreams, that I may give
Pulse for pulse, breath for breath:
Speak low, lean low,
As long ago, my love, how long ago.

– *Christina Rossetti*

Beautiful Dreamer

Beautiful dreamer, wake unto me,
Starlight and dewdrops are waiting for thee;
Sounds of the rude world heard in the day,
Lulled by the moonlight have all passed away!

Beautiful dreamer, queen of my song,
List while I woo thee with soft melody;
Gone are the cares of life's busy throng.
Beautiful dreamer, awake unto me!

Beautiful dreamer, out on the sea,
Mermaids are chanting the wild lorelie[1];
Over the streamlet vapours are borne,
Waiting to fade at the bright coming morn.

Beautiful dreamer, beam on my heart,
E'en as the morn on the streamlet and sea;
Then will all clouds of sorrow depart,
Beautiful dreamer, awake unto me!

— *Stephen Foster*

---

1 lorelie – a song to lure men to destruction

Sentimental Me

Look at me again, dear;
let's hold hands, and then, dear
sigh in chorus; it won't bore us, to be sure.
There's no meaning to it
yet we overdo it,
with a relish that is hellish to endure;
I am not the kind that merely flirts –
I just love and love until it hurts.

Darling you're so handsome –
strong and clever – and sometimes you seem, dear,
like a dream, dear, that came true.
That's why I picked you out.
Better men I threw out
of my living room while giving room to you.
I would rather read of love in books;
Love is much more painful than it looks.

Oh, sentimental me and poor romantic you!
Dreaming dreams is all that we can do.
We hang around all day and ponder,

while both of us grow fonder –
the Lord knows where we're wandering to!
I sit and sigh; you sigh and sit upon my knee;
we laugh and cry, and never disagree;
a million kisses we'll make theft of
until there's nothing left of
poor romantic you and sentimental me.

– *Lorenz Hart*

Ballade Of The Devil-May-Care

Free as the wandering pike am I,
    Many the strings to my amorous bow,
More than a little inclined to fly
    Butterfly lovering[1], to and fro;
    Happy wherever the flowers blow,
With the dew on the leaf, and the sunshine above.
    Terribly wrong and unprincipled?
No, Life is too short to be 'dead in love!'

Not for me is the lover's sigh;
    Fools are they, to be worrying so!
Sipping my fill of the honey I fly
    Butterfly lovering, to and fro.
I skim the cream, and let all else go;
    Gather my roses, and give a shove
Over my shoulder at dutiful woe, –
    Life is too short to be 'dead in love!'

---

[1] lovering – love-making

So, while the fanciful hours go by,
    I gaily reap what the simpletons sow.
Fresh with their bloom are the fruits I try,
    Butterfly lovering, to and fro.
    Then here's to the lady who wears her beau
On and off, like a dainty glove!
    And here's to the zephyrs that all-ways blow –
Life is too short to be 'dead in love!'

Prince, who cares for the coming snow,
    Butterfly lovering, to and fro?
Why should a man be a turtle-dove?
Life is too short to be 'dead in love!'

– *Gelett Burgess*

Dream Land

When in my dreams thy lovely face,
Smiles with unwonted tender grace,
Grudge not the precious seldom cheer;
I know full well, my lady dear! It is no boon of thine.

In thy sweet sanctuary of sleep,
If my sad sprite should kneeling weep,
Suffer its speechless worship there;
Thou know'st full well, my lady fair! It is no fault
   of mine.

— *Frances Anne Kemble*

No Longer Jealous

I remember the time ere his temples were grey,
And I frowned at the things he'd the boldness to say,
But now he's grown old, he may say what he will,
I laugh at his nonsense and take nothing ill.

Indeed I must say he's a little improved,
For he watches no longer the 'slily beloved,'
No longer as once he awakens my fears,
Not a glance he perceives, not a whisper he hears.

If he heard one of late, it has never transpired,
For his only delight is to see me admired;
And now pray what better return can I make,
Than to flirt and be always admired – for his sake?

– *Walter Savage Landor*

Annabel Lee

It was many and many a year ago,
In a kingdom by the sea,
That a maiden there lived whom you may know
By the name of Annabel Lee;
And this maiden she lived with no other thought
Than to love and be loved by me.

She was a child and I was a child,
In this kingdom by the sea,
But we loved with a love that was more than love –
I and my Annabel Lee –
With a love that the winged seraphs of heaven
Coveted her and me.

And this was the reason that, long ago,
In this kingdom by the sea,
A wind blew out of a cloud by night
Chilling my Annabel Lee;
So that her high-born kinsman came

And bore her away from me,
To shut her up in a sepulchre
In this kingdom by the sea.

The angels, not half so happy in Heaven,
Went envying her and me:
Yes! that was the reason (as all men know,
In this kingdom by the sea)
That the wind came out of a cloud, chilling
And killing my Annabel Lee.

But our love it was stronger by far than the love
Of those who were older than we –
Of many far wiser than we –
And neither the angels in Heaven above,
Nor the demons down under the sea,
Can ever dissever my soul from the soul
Of the beautiful Annabel Lee:

For the moon never beams without bringing me dreams
Of the beautiful Annabel Lee;
And the stars never rise but I see the bright eyes
Of the beautiful Annabel Lee;
And so, all the night-tide, I lie down by the side
Of my darling, my darling, my life and my bride,
In her sepulchre there by the sea –
In her tomb by the side of the sea.

– *Edgar Allan Poe*

Somewhere Or Other

Somewhere or other there must surely be
The face not seen, the voice not heard,
The heart that not yet – never yet – ah me!
Made answer to my word.

Somewhere or other, may be near or far;
Past land and sea, clean out of sight;
Beyond the wandering moon, beyond the star
That tracks her night by night.

Somewhere or other, may be far or near;
With just a wall, a hedge, between;
With just the last leaves of the dying year
Fallen on a turf grown green.

– *Christina Rossetti*

Trust Thou Thy Love

Trust thou thy Love: if she be proud, is she not sweet?
Trust thou thy Love: if she be mute, is she not pure?
Lay thou thy soul full in her hands, low at her feet;
Fail, Sun and Breath! – yet, for thy peace, She shall endure.

– *John Ruskin*

Precious To Me

Precious to me – she still shall be –
Though she forget the name I bear –
The fashion of the gown I wear –
The very colour of my hair –

So like the meadows – now –
I dared to show a tress of theirs
If haply – she might not despise
A buttercup's array –

I know the whole – obscures the part –
The fraction – that appeased the heart
Till number's empery –
Remembered – as the millner's flower

When Summer's everlasting dower –
Confronts the dazzled bee.

– *Emily Dickinson*

Rosalind's Madrigal

Love in my bosom like a bee
    Doth suck his sweet;
Now with his wings he plays with me,
    Now with his feet.
Within mine eyes he makes his nest,
His bed amidst my tender breast;
My kisses are his daily feast,
And yet he robs me of my rest.
    Ah, wanton, will ye?

And if I sleep, then percheth he
    With pretty flight,
And makes his pillow of my knee
    The livelong night.
Strike I my lute, he tunes the string;
He music plays if so I sing;
He lends me every lovely thing;
Yet cruel he my heart doth sting.
    Whist, wanton, still ye!

Else I with roses every day
    Will whip you hence,
And bind you, when you long to play,
    For your offense.
I'll shut mine eyes to keep you in,
I'll make you fast it for your sin,
I'll count your power not worth a pin.
Alas! what hereby shall I win
    If he gainsay me?

What if I beat the wanton boy
    With many a rod?
He will repay me with annoy,
    Because a god.
Then sit thou safely on my knee,
And let thy bower my bosom be;
Lurk in mine eyes, I like of thee.
O Cupid, so thou pity me,
    Spare not, but play thee!

— *Thomas Lodge*

To Any One

♎

Whether the time be slow or fast,
    Enemies, hand in hand,
Must come together at the last
    And understand.

No matter how the die is cast
    Nor who may seem to win,
You know that you must love at last —
    Why not begin?

— *Witter Bynner*

Love's Blindness

They call her fair. I do not know:
    I never thought to look.
Who heeds the binder's costliest show
    When he may read the book?

What need a list of parts to me
    When I possess the whole?
Who only watch her eyes to see
    The colour of her soul.

I may not praise her mouth, her chin,
    Her feet, her hands, her arms:
My love lacks leisure to begin
    The schedule of her charms.

To praise is only to compare:
    And therefore Love is blind.
I loved before I was aware
    Her beauty was of kind.

– *William James Linton*

If Women Could Be Fair And Yet Not Fond

If women could be fair and yet not fond,
    Or that their love were firm, not fickle still,
I would not marvel that they make men bond
    By service long to purchase their good will;
But when I see how frail those creatures are,
I laugh that men forget themselves so far.

To mark the choice they make, and how they change,
    How oft from Phoebus do they flee to Pan;
Unsettled still, like haggards[1] wild they range,
    These gentle birds that fly from man to man;
Who would not scorn and shake them from the fist,
And let them fly, fair fools, which way they list?

---

1 haggards – wild-looking birds

Yet for our sport we fawn and flatter both,
   To pass the time when nothing else can please,
And train them to our lure with subtle oath,
   Till, weary of their wiles, ourselves we ease;
And then we say when we their fancy try,
To play with fools, O what a fool was I!

— *Edward de Vere*

Spring Song

♎

Ah love, the sweet spring blossoms cling
To many a broken wind-tossed bough,
And young birds among branches sing
That mutely hung till now.

The little new-born things which lie
In dewy meadows, sleep and dream
Beside the brook that twinkles by
To some great lonely stream.

And children, now the day is told,
From many a warm and cosy nest,
Look up to see the young moon hold
The old moon to her breast.

Dear love, my pulses throb and start
To-night with longings sweet and new,
And young hopes beat within a heart
Grown old in loving you.

– Dollie Radford

Love Came Knocking

Love came knocking at my door in the flowery month
   of May,
'Twas the morning of the year, and the morning of the
   day;
   He was a winsome boy,
   And I a maiden coy,
But I followed him, I followed! for he drew me with
   the wile
Of his eyes, his words, and whispers, and the glamour
   of his smile.

Oh the merry laughing moments, oh the soft, the
   shining hours,
When I followed as he led me through his gardens and
   his bowers!
   Love was a thing divine,
   I was his, and he was mine;
So I followed him, I followed, could have followed till
   I died,
In the wake of his young glory, and the fullness of my
   pride.

Now the merry days are over, with the joy and pride
   and show;
Love has grown to his full stature; I am weary as I go.
      Shamed is the golden head,
      And the magic smile is fled
      For the dust and soil of earth
      Mock the greatness of Love's birth;
But I follow, and if weeping I, though weeping, follow
   still,
With no magic and no glamour, but a faithful human
   will.

Ay, I follow still, I follow, though no longer through
   the May,
Though the lingering dreams of morning with the
   morn have passed away.
      Now Love is no more glad,
      Nay, his very smile is sad;
      But he needs me even more
      Than I needed him before;
So I follow, still I follow, and through all the darker
   seeming,
Love's true need of me is sweeter than his smile that
   held me dreaming.

And when one day hand in hand we before God's gate shall stand,
And the gate shall open wide that we enter side by side,
    We may gaze in glad surprise
    Into one another's eyes,
    Not to find a winsome boy,
    Or a maiden vain and coy;
    But two creatures shining bright
    In the pure and keen love-light,
    Of the patience and the faith
    That have conquered more than death.
Then I follow love no longer, but I sink upon thy breast
To abide there hushed for ever in the joy of utter rest.

– Emily Pfeiffer

Estrangement

So, without overt breach, we fall apart,
Tacitly sunder – neither you nor I
Conscious of one intelligible Why,
And both, from severance, winning equal smart.
So, with resigned and acquiescent heart,
Whene'er your name on some chance lip may lie,
I seem to see an alien shade pass by,
A spirit wherein I have no lot or part.
Thus may a captive, in some fortress grim,
From casual speech betwixt his warders, learn
That June on her triumphant progress goes
Through arched and bannered woodlands; while for him
She is a legend emptied of concern,
And idle is the rumour of the rose.

– William Watson

A Long, Long Kiss

And thus they wandered forth, and hand in hand,
    Over the shining pebbles and the shells,
Glided along the smooth and hardened sand,
    And in the worn and wild receptacles
Worked by the storms, yet worked as it were planned,
    In hollow halls, with sparry roofs and cells,
They turned to rest; and, each clasped by an arm,
Yielded to the deep twilight's purple charm.

They looked up to the sky, whose floating glow
    Spread like a rosy ocean, vast and bright;
They gazed upon the glittering sea below,
    Whence the broad moon rose circling into sight;
They heard the wave's splash, and the wind so low,
    And saw each other's dark eyes darting light
Into each other – and, beholding this,
Their lips drew near, and clung into a kiss;

A long, long kiss, a kiss of youth, and love,
    And beauty, all concentrating like rays
Into one focus, kindled from above;
    Such kisses as belong to early days,
Where heart, and soul, and sense, in concert move,
    And the blood's lava, and the pulse a blaze,
Each kiss a heart-quake, – for a kiss's strength,
I think, it must be reckoned by its length.

By length I mean duration; theirs endured
    Heaven knows how long – no doubt they never reckoned;
And if they had, they could not have secured
    The sum of their sensations to a second:
They had not spoken; but they felt allured,
    As if their souls and lips each other beckoned,
Which, being joined, like swarming bees they clung –
Their hearts the flowers from whence the honey sprung.

They were alone, but not alone as they
    Who shut in chambers think it loneliness;
The silent ocean, and the starlight bay,
    The twilight glow which momently grew less,
The voiceless sands and dropping caves, that lay
    Around them, made them to each other press,
As if there were no life beneath the sky
Save theirs, and that their life could never die.

They feared no eyes nor ears on that lone beach,
    They felt no terrors from the night, they were
All in all to each other: though their speech
    Was broken words, they *thought* a language there, –
And all the burning tongues the passions teach
    Found in one sigh the best interpreter
Of nature's oracle – first love, – that all
Which Eve has left her daughters since her fall.

– *Lord Byron*

The Lonely Maid

Can anyone tell what I ail
That I look so lean, so wan, so pale?
Unto that plight, alas, I'm grown
That can, nor will, no longer lie alone.

Was ever woman's case like mine?
At fifteen I began to pine;
So now unto this plight I'm grown
That can, nor will, no longer lie alone.

If dreams be true, then ride I can –
I lack nothing but a man.
For only he can ease my moan
That can, nor will, no longer lie alone.

When day is come, I wish for night;
When night is come, I wish for light;
Thus all my time I sit and moan
That can, nor will, no longer lie alone.

To woo him first, ashamed am I;
But if he ask, I'll not deny –
Such is my case, I must have one
That can, nor will, no longer lie alone.

Therefore my prayer, it shall be still
I may have one to work my will,
For only he can ease me anon,
That can, nor will, no longer lie alone.

– Anon

Meditation For His Mistress

You are a tulip seen to-day,
But, dearest, of so short a stay
That where you grew scarce man can say.

You are a lovely July-flower,
Yet one rude wind or ruffling shower
Will force you hence, and in an hour.

You are a sparkling rose i' th' bud,
Yet lost ere that chaste flesh and blood
Can show where you or grew or stood.

You are a full-spread, fair-set vine,
And can with tendrils love entwine,
Yet dried ere you distil your wine.

You are like balm enclosed well
In amber, or some crystal shell,
Yet lost ere you transfuse your smell.

You are a dainty violet,
Yet withered ere you can be set
Within the virgin's coronet.

You are the queen all flowers among,
But die you must, fair maid, ere long,
As he, the maker of this song.

– *Robert Herrick*

The Cap And Bells

The jester walked in the garden:
The garden had fallen still;
He bade his soul rise upward
And stand on her window-sill.

It rose in a straight blue garment,
When owls began to call:
It had grown wise-tongued by thinking
Of a quiet and light footfall;

But the young queen would not listen;
She rose in her pale night-gown;
She drew in the heavy casement
And pushed the latches down.

He bade his heart go to her,
When the owls called out no more;
In a red and quivering garment
It sang to her through the door.

It had grown sweet-tongued by dreaming
Of a flutter of flower-like hair;
But she took up her fan from the table
And waved it off on the air.

'I have cap and bells,' he pondered,
'I will send them to her and die';
And when the morning whitened
He left them where she went by.

She laid them upon her bosom,
Under a cloud of her hair,
And her red lips sang them a love-song
Till stars grew out of the air.

She opened her door and her window,
And the heart and the soul came through,
To her right hand came the red one,
To her left hand came the blue.

They set up a noise like crickets,
A chattering wise and sweet,
And her hair was a folded flower
And the quiet of love in her feet.

– *W. B. Yeats*

Ruth

♎

She stood breast high amid the corn,
Clasped by the golden light of morn,
Like the sweetheart of the sun,
Who many a glowing kiss had won.

On her cheek an autumn flush,
Deeply ripened; – such a blush
In the midst of brown was born,
Like red poppies grown with corn.

Round her eyes her tresses fell,
Which were blackest none could tell,
But long lashes veiled a light,
That had else been all too bright.

And her hat, with shady brim,
Made her tressy forehead dim; –
Thus she stood amid the stooks,
Praising God with sweetest looks: –

Sure, I said, heaven did not mean,
Where I reap thou shouldst but glean,
Lay thy sheaf adown and come,
Share my harvest and my home.

– *Thomas Hood*

She Walks In Beauty

She walks in beauty, like the night
Of cloudless climes and starry skies;
And all that's best of dark and bright
Meet in her aspect and her eyes:
Thus mellowed to that tender light
Which heaven to gaudy day denies.

One shade the more, one ray the less,
Had half impaired the nameless grace
Which waves in every raven tress,
Or softly lightens o'er her face;
Where thoughts serenely sweet express
How pure, how dear their dwelling-place.

And on that cheek, and o'er that brow,
So soft, so calm, yet eloquent,
The smiles that win, the tints that glow,
But tell of days in goodness spent,
A mind at peace with all content
A heart whose love is innocent!

– *Lord Byron*

Go, Lovely Rose

Go, lovely rose!
Tell her that wastes her time and me
That now she knows,
When I resemble her to thee,
How sweet and fair she seems to be.

Tell her that's young,
And shuns to have her graces spied,
That hadst thou sprung
In deserts, where no men abide,
Thou must have uncommended died.

Small is the worth
Of beauty from the light retired;
Bid her come forth,
Suffer herself to be desired,
And not blush so to be admired.

Then die! that she
The common fate of all things rare
May read in thee;
How small a part of time they share
That are so wondrous sweet and fair!

– Edmund Waller

The Anniversary

All kings, and all their favourites,
All glory of honours, beauties, wits,
The sun it self, which makes time, as they pass,
Is elder by a year now than it was
When thou and I first one another saw.
All other things to their destruction draw,
Only our love hath no decay;
This no to-morrow hath, nor yesterday;
Running it never runs from us away,
But truly keeps his first, last, everlasting day.

Two graves must hide thine and my corpse;
If one might, death were no divorce.
Alas! as well as other princes, we
– Who prince enough in one another be –
Must leave at last in death these eyes and ears,
Oft fed with true oaths, and with sweet salt tears;

But souls where nothing dwells but love
– All other thoughts being inmates – then shall prove
This or a love increasèd there above,
When bodies to their graves, souls from their graves remove.

And then we shall be throughly blest;
But now no more than all the rest.
Here upon earth we're kings, and none but we
Can be such kings, nor of such subjects be.

Who is so safe as we? where none can do
Treason to us, except one of us two.
True and false fears let us refrain,
Let us love nobly, and live, and add again
Years and years unto years, till we attain
To write threescore; this is the second of our reign.

– John Donne

Aedh Gives His Beloved Certain Rhymes

Fasten your hair with a golden pin,
And bind up every wandering tress;
I bade my heart build these poor rhymes:
It worked at them, day out, day in,
Building a sorrowful loveliness
Out of the battles of old times.

You need but lift a pearl-pale hand,
And bind up your long hair and sigh;
And all men's hearts must burn and beat;
And candle-like foam on the dim sand,
And stars climbing the dew-dropping sky,
Live but to light your passing feet.

– W. B. Yeats

The Dance

As the Wind, and as the Wind,
    In a corner of the way,
Goes stepping, stands twirling,
Invisibly, comes whirling,
Bows before, and skips behind,
    In a grave, an endless play –

So my Heart, and so my Heart,
    Following where your feet have gone,
Stirs dust of old dreams there;
He turns a toe; he gleams there,
Treading you a dance apart.
    But you see not. You pass on.

– *Rupert Brooke*

Margaret

Mother, I cannot mind my wheel;
My fingers ache, my lips are dry;
Oh, if you felt the pain I feel!
But oh, who ever felt as I!

No longer could I doubt him true,
All other men may use deceit;
He always said my eyes were blue,
And often swore my lips were sweet.

– *Walter Savage Landor*

So, We'll Go No More A-Roving

So, we'll go no more a-roving
    So late into the night,
Though the heart be still as loving,
    And the moon be still as bright.

For the sword outwears its sheath,
    And the soul wears out the breast,
And the heart must pause to breathe,
    And love itself have rest.

Though the night was made for loving,
    And the day returns too soon,
Yet we'll go no more a-roving
    By the light of the moon.

— Lord Byron

When I Was Fair And Young

When I was fair and young then favour graced me;
Of many was I sought their mistress for to be.
But I did scorn them all, and answered them therefore,
Go, go, go, seek some otherwhere,
Importune me no more.

How many weeping eyes I made to pine in woe;
How many sighing hearts I have no skill to show;
Yet I the prouder grew, and answered them therefore,
Go, go, go, seek some otherwhere,
Importune me no more.

Then spake fair Venus' son, that proud victorious boy,
And said, you dainty dame, since that you be so coy,
I will so pluck your plumes that you shall say no more
Go, go, go, seek some otherwhere,
Importune me no more.

When he had spake these words such change grew in
    my breast,
That neither night nor day I could take any rest.
Then, lo! I did repent, that I had said before
Go, go, go, seek some otherwhere,
Importune me no more.

— Perhaps Queen Elizabeth I

To Jane, With A Guitar

♎

The keen stars were twinkling,
And the fair moon was rising among them,
Dear Jane!
The guitar was tinkling,
But the notes were not sweet till you sung them
Again.

As the moon's soft splendour
O'er the faint cold starlight of Heaven
Is thrown,
So your voice most tender
To the strings without soul had then given
Its own.

The stars will awaken,
Though the moon sleep a full hour later,
To-night;
No leaf will be shaken
Whilst the dews of your melody scatter
Delight.

Though the sound overpowers,
Sing again, with your dear voice revealing
A tone
Of some world far from ours,
Where music and moonlight and feeling
Are one.

– *Percy Bysshe Shelley*

For Music

There be none of Beauty's daughters
    With a magic like thee;
And like music on the waters
    Is thy sweet voice to me:
    When, as if its sound were causing
The charmèd ocean's pausing,
The waves lie still and gleaming,
And the lulled winds seem dreaming:

And the midnight moon is weaving
    Her bright chain o'er the deep;
Whose breast is gently heaving,
    As an infant's asleep:
So the spirit bows before thee,
To listen and adore thee;
With a full but soft emotion,
Like the swell of Summer's ocean.

– *Lord Byron*

The Master Chord

Like a musician that with flying finger
Startles the voice of some new instrument,
And, though he know that in one string are blent
All its extremes of sound, yet still doth linger
Among the lighter threads, fearing to start
The deep soul of that one melodious wire,
Lest it, unanswering, dash his high desire,
And spoil the hopes of his expectant heart;
Thus, with my mistress oft conversing, I
Stir every lighter theme with careless voice,
Gathering sweet music and celestial joys
From the harmonious soul o'er which I fly;
Yet o'er the one deep master-chord I hover,
And dare not stoop, fearing to tell – I love her.

– *William Caldwell Roscoe*

Music, When Soft Voices Die

Music, when soft voices die,
Vibrates in the memory –
Odours, when sweet violets sicken,
Live within the sense they quicken.

Rose leaves, when the rose is dead,
Are heaped for the beloved's bed;
And so thy thoughts when thou are gone,
Love itself shall slumber on.

– P. B. Shelley

Julia's Voice

So smooth, so sweet, so silvery is thy voice
As, could they hear, the damned would make no noise,
But listen to thee, walking in thy chamber,
Melting melodious words to lutes of amber.

— *Robert Herrick*

An Elegy On The Glory Of Her Sex, Mrs Mary Blaize

♎

Good people all, with one accord
Lament for Madam Blaize,
Who never wanted a good word,
From those who spoke her praise.

The needy seldom passed her door,
And always found her kind;
She freely lent to all the poor,
Who left a pledge behind.

She strove the neighbourhood to please
With manners wondrous winning;
And never followed wicked ways,
Unless when she was sinning.

At church, in silks and satins new,
With hoop of monstrous size,
She never slumbered in her pew,
But when she shut her eyes.

Her love was sought, I do aver,
By twenty beaux and more;
The king himself has followed her,
When she has walked before.

But now her wealth and finery fled,
Her hangers-on cut short all;
The doctors found, when she was dead,
Her last disorder mortal.

Let us lament in sorrow sore,
For Kent Street well may say
That had she lived a twelvemonth more,
She had not died today.

– *Oliver Goldsmith*

The Suburbs

Miles and miles of quiet houses, every house a harbour,
Each for some unquiet soul a haven and a home,
Pleasant fires for winter nights, for sun the trellised arbour,
Earth the solid underfoot, and heaven for a dome.

Washed by storms of cleansing rain, and sweetened with affliction,
The hidden wells of Love are heard in one low-murmuring voice
That rises from this close-meshed life so like a benediction
That, listening to it, in my heart I almost dare rejoice.

– Enid Derham

Wattle And Myrtle

Gold of the tangled wilderness of wattle,
   Break in the lone green hollows of the hills,
Flame on the iron headlands of the ocean,
   Gleam on the margin of the hurrying rills.

Come with thy saffron diadem and scatter
   Odours of Araby that haunt the air,
Queen of our woodland, rival of the roses,
   Spring in the yellow tresses of thy hair.

Surely the old gods, dwellers on Olympus,
   Under thy shining loveliness have strayed,
Crowned with thy clusters, magical Apollo,
   Pan with his reedy music may have played.

Surely within thy fastness, Aphrodite,
   She of the sea-ways, fallen from above,
Wandered beneath thy canopy of blossom,
   Nothing disdainful of a mortal's love.

Aye, and Her sweet breath lingers on the wattle,
    Aye, and Her myrtle dominates the glade,
And with a deep and perilous enchantment
    Melts in the heart of lover and of maid.

— *James Lister Cuthbertson*

Love And Music

I listened to the music broad and deep:
I heard the tenor in an ecstasy
Touch the sweet, distant goal; I heard the cry
Of prayer and passion; and I heard the sweep
Of mighty wings, that in their waving keep
The music that the spheres make endlessly; –
Then my cheek shivered, tears made blind mine eye;
As flame to flame I felt the quick blood leap,
And, through the tides and moonlit winds of sound,
To me love's passionate voice grew audible.
Again I felt thy heart to my heart bound,
Then silence on the viols and voices fell;
But, like the still, small voice within a shell,
I heard Love thrilling through the void profound.

– *Philip Bourke Marston*

From Spring Days To Winter

In the glad springtime when leaves were green,
O merrily the throstle[1] sings!
I sought, amid the tangled sheen,
Love whom mine eyes had never seen,
O the glad dove has golden wings!

Between the blossoms red and white,
O merrily the throstle sings!
My love first came into my sight,
O perfect vision of delight,
O the glad dove has golden wings!

The yellow apples glowed like fire,
O merrily the throstle sings!
O Love too great for lip or lyre,
Blown rose of love and of desire,
O the glad dove has golden wings!

---
1 throstle – thrush

But now with snow the tree is grey,
Ah, sadly now the throstle sings!
My love is dead: ah! well-a-day,
See at her silent feet I lay
A dove with broken wings!
Ah, Love! ah, Love! that thou wert slain –
Fond Dove, fond Dove return again!

– *Oscar Wilde*

Swallow, Swallow

Swallow, swallow, neighbour swallow,
Starting on your autumn flight,
Pause a moment at my window,
Twitter softly your good-night;
For the summer days are over,
All your duties are well done,
And the happy homes you builded
Have grown empty, one by one.

Swallow, swallow, neighbour swallow,
Are you ready for your flight?
Are all the feather cloaks completed?
Are the little caps all right?
Are the young wings strong and steady
For the journey through the sky?
Come again in early spring-time;
And till then, good-by, good-by!

– *Louisa May Alcott*

Song

The linnet in the rocky dells,
The moor-lark in the air,
The bee among the heather bells
That hide my lady fair:

The wild deer browse above her breast;
The wild birds raise their brood;
And they, her smiles of love caressed,
Have left her solitude!

I ween, that when the grave's dark wall
Did first her form retain,
They thought their hearts could ne'er recall
The light of joy again.

They thought the tide of grief would flow
Unchecked through future years;
But where is all their anguish now,
And where are all their tears?

Well, let them fight for honour's breath,
Or pleasure's shade pursue –
The dweller in the land of death
Is changed and careless too.

And, if their eyes should watch and weep
Till sorrow's source were dry,
She would not, in her tranquil sleep,
Return a single sigh!

Blow, west-wind, by the lonely mound,
And murmur, summer-streams –
There is no need of other sound
To soothe my lady's dreams.

– *Emily Brontë*

Love Me At Last

♎

Love me at last, or if you will not,
Leave me;
Hard words could never, as these half-words,
Grieve me:
Love me at last – or leave me.
Love me at last, or let the last word uttered
Be but your own;
Love me, or leave me – as a cloud, a vapour,
Or a bird flown.
Love me at last – I am but sliding water
Over a stone.

– Alice Corbin

Love's Philosophy

The fountains mingle with the river,
And the rivers with the ocean;
The winds of heaven mix forever
With a sweet emotion;
Nothing in the world is single;
All things by a law divine
In another's being mingle –
Why not I with thine?

See, the mountains kiss high heaven,
And the waves clasp one another;
No sister flower could be forgiven
If it disdained its brother;
And the sunlight clasps the earth,
And the moonbeams kiss the sea; –
What are all these kissings worth,
If thou kiss not me?

– *Percy Bysshe Shelley*

Sad Is That Woman's Lot

Sad is that woman's lot who, year by year,
Sees, one by one, her beauties disappear,
When Time, grown weary of her heart-drawn sighs,
Impatiently begins to 'dim her eyes!'
Compelled, at last, in life's uncertain gloamings,
To wreathe her wrinkled brow with well-saved
    'combings',
Reduced, with rouge, lip-salve, and pearly grey,
To 'make up' for lost time as best she may!

Silvered is the raven hair,
    Spreading is the parting straight,
Mottled the complexion fair,
    Halting is the youthful gait,
Hollow is the laughter free,
    Spectacled the limpid eye,
Little will be left of me
    In the coming bye and bye!

Fading is the taper waist,
    Shapeless grows the shapely limb,
And although severely laced,
    Spreading is the figure trim!
Stouter than I used to be,
    Still more corpulent grow I –
There will be too much of me
    In the coming by-and-bye!

– *W. S. Gilbert*

The Bluebell

A fine and subtle spirit dwells
In every little flower,
Each one its own sweet feeling breathes
With more or less of power.

There is a silent eloquence
In every wild bluebell
That fills my softened heart with bliss
That words could never tell.

Yet I recall not long ago
A bright and sunny day,
'Twas when I led a toilsome life
So many leagues away;

That day along a sunny road
All carelessly I strayed,
Between two banks where smiling flowers
Their varied hues displayed.

Before me rose a lofty hill,
Behind me lay the sea,
My heart was not so heavy then
As it was wont to be.

Less harassed than at other times
I saw the scene was fair,
And spoke and laughed to those around,
As if I knew no care.

But when I looked upon the bank
My wandering glances fell
Upon a little trembling flower,
A single sweet bluebell.

Whence came that rising in my throat,
That dimness in my eye?
Why did those burning drops distil –
Those bitter feelings rise?

O, that lone flower recalled to me
My happy childhood's hours
When bluebells seemed like fairy gifts
A prize among the flowers,

Those sunny days of merriment
When heart and soul were free,
And when I dwelt with kindred hearts
That loved and cared for me.

I had not then mid heartless crowds
To spend a thankless life
In seeking after others' weal
With anxious toil and strife.

'Sad wanderer, weep those blissful times
That never may return!'
The lovely floweret seemed to say,
And thus it made me mourn.

– *Emily Brontë*

Autumn Fires

In the other gardens
And all up the vale,
From the autumn bonfires
See the smoke trail!

Pleasant summer over
And all the summer flowers,
The red fire blazes,
The grey smoke towers.

Sing a song of seasons!
Something bright in all!
Flowers in the summer,
Fires in the fall!

– *Robert Louis Stevenson*

September In Australia

Grey Winter hath gone, like a wearisome guest,
    And, behold, for repayment,
September comes in with the wind of the West
    And the Spring in her raiment!
The ways of the frost have been filled of the flowers,
    While the forest discovers
Wild wings, with a halo of hyaline hours,
    And a music of lovers.

September, the maid with the swift, silver feet!
    She glides, and she graces
The valleys of coolness, the slopes of the heat,
    With her blossomy traces;
Sweet month, with a mouth that is made of a rose,
    She lightens and lingers
In spots where the harp of the evening glows,
    Attuned by her fingers.

The stream from its home in the hollow hill slips
    In a darling old fashion;
And the day goeth down with a song on its lips

  Whose key-note is passion.
Far out in the fierce, bitter front of the sea
  I stand, and remember
Dead things that were brothers and sisters of thee,
  Resplendent September.

The West, when it blows at the fall of the noon
  And beats on her beaches,
So filled with a tender and tremulous tune
  That touches and teaches;
The stories of Youth, of the burden of Time,
  And the death of Devotion
Come back with the wind, and are themes of the rhyme
  In the waves of the ocean.

We, having a secret to others unknown,
  In the cool mountain-mosses,
May whisper together, September, alone
  Of our loves and our losses.
One word for her beauty, and one for the grace
  She gave to the hours;
And then we may kiss her, and suffer her face
  To sleep with the flowers.

High places that knew of the gold and the white
  On the forehead of Morning
Now darken and quake, and the steps of the Night
  Are heavy with warning!
Her voice in the distance is lofty and loud
  Through its echoing gorges;

She hath hidden her eyes in a mantle of cloud,
    And her feet in the surges!

On the tops of the hills, on the turreted cones –
    Chief temples of thunder –
The gale, like a ghost, in the middle watch moans,
    Gliding over and under.
The sea, flying white through the rack and the rain,
    Leapeth wild at the forelands;
And the plover, whose cry is like passion with pain,
    Complains in the moorlands.

Oh, season of changes – of shadow and shine –
    September the splendid!
My song hath no music to mingle with thine,
    And its burden is ended;
But thou, being born of the winds and the sun,
    By mountain, by river,
Mayst lighten and listen, and loiter and run,
    With thy voices for ever.

– Adam Lindsay Gordon

October

Ay, thou art welcome, heaven's delicious breath,
    When woods begin to wear the crimson leaf,
    And suns grow meek, and the meek suns grow brief,
And the year smiles as it draws near its death.
Wind of the sunny south! oh still delay
    In the gay woods and in the golden air,
    Like to a good old age released from care,
Journeying, in long serenity, away.
In such a bright, late quiet, would that I
    Might wear out life like thee, mid bowers and brooks,
    And, dearer yet, the sunshine of kind looks,
And music of kind voices ever nigh;
And when my last sand twinkled in the glass,
Pass silently from men, as thou dost pass.

— *William Cullen Bryant*

A Myth

♎

A-floating, a-floating
Across the sleeping sea,
All night I heard a singing bird
Upon the topmast tree.

'Oh, came you from the isles of Greece
Or from the banks of Seine;
Or off some tree in forests free,
Which fringe the western main?'

'I came not off the old world
Nor yet from off the new –
But I am one of the birds of God
Which sing the whole night through.'

'Oh, sing and wake the dawning –
Oh, whistle for the wind;
The night is long, the current strong,
My boat it lags behind.'

'The current sweeps the old world,
The current sweeps the new;
The wind will blow, the dawn will glow,
Ere thou hast sail'd them through.'

– *Charles Kingsley*

The Flatterers

♎

The cactus has grown young leaves
One and a half inches long
Since I came to live with it.
Its branches are like the claws of crabs
In a bed of seaweed.
Young rose-hued shoots are coming
From the new green leaves.
I have divined their desires.
They would make huge boughs
Of soft green for you and me
To sit under,
And tell each other of ourselves
And of the world.

Outside the wall of this room,
The young tamarisk tree waves
Its feathery grey branches in the wind.
It has sent its coral-dust blossoms to the ground.
They were like wafts of smoke from a tepee
In the morning just before the sun
Reaches the desert.

I sat one evening in the moonlight,
Under the tamarisk tree,
And listened to songs from the lips
Of a Mexican boy.

He told me afterward in broken English
The meaning of these songs.
I could have told him a richer meaning.
I could have told him of your presence
Inside the wall of this room.
I told him nothing of your presence.
It is enough the cactus and the tamarisk are knowing,

– *Marsden Hartley*

Sunday Up The River

My love o'er the water bends dreaming;
    It glideth and glideth away:
She sees there her own beauty, gleaming
    Through shadow and ripple and spray.

O tell her, thou murmuring river,
    As past her your light wavelets roll,
How steadfast that image for ever
    Shines pure in pure depths of my soul.

– James Thomson

To The Gossamer Light

Quick gleam, that ridest on the gossamer!
How oft I see thee, with thy wavering lance,
Tilt at the midges in their evening dance,
A gentle joust set on by summer air!
How oft I watch thee from my garden chair!
And, failing that, I search the lawns and bowers,
To find thee floating o'er the fruits and flowers,
And doing thy sweet work in silence there.
Thou art the poet's darling, ever sought
In the fair garden or the breezy mead;
The wind dismounts thee not; thy buoyant thread
Is as the sonnet, poising one bright thought,
That moves but does not vanish: borne along
Like light, – a golden drift through all the song.

– *Charles Tennyson Turner*

La Fuite De La Lune

To outer senses there is peace,
A dreamy peace on either hand,
Deep silence in the shadowy land,
Deep silence where the shadows cease.

Save for a cry that echoes shrill
From some lone bird disconsolate;
A corncrake calling to its mate;
The answer from the misty hill.

And suddenly the moon withdraws
Her sickle from the lightening skies,
And to her sombre cavern flies,
Wrapped in a veil of yellow gauze.

— *Oscar Wilde*

Song

♎

Rarely, rarely comest thou,
    Spirit of Delight!
Wherefore hast thou left me now
    Many a day and night?
Many a weary night and day
'Tis since thou art fled away.

How shall ever one like me
    Win thee back again?
With the joyous and the free
    Thou wilt scoff at pain.
Spirit false! thou hast forgot
All but those who need thee not.

As a lizard with the shade
    Of a trembling leaf,
Thou with sorrow art dismayed;
    Even the sighs of grief
Reproach thee, that thou art not near,
And reproach thou wilt not her.

Let me set my mournful ditty
    To a merry measure; –
Thou wilt never come for pity,
    Thou wilt come for pleasure;
Pity then will cut away
Those cruel wings, and thou wilt stay.

I love all that thou lovest,
    Spirit of Delight!
The fresh Earth in new leaves dressed,
    And the starry night;
Autumn evening, and the morn
When the golden mists are born.

I love snow and all the forms
    Of the radiant frost;
I love waves, and winds, and storms,
    Everything almost
Which is Nature's, and may be
Untainted by man's misery.

I love tranquil solitude,
    And such society
As is quiet, wise, and good;
    Between thee and me
What difference? but thou dost possess
The things I seek, not love them less.

I love Love – though he has wings,
    And like light can flee,
But above all other things,
    Spirit, I love thee –
Thou art love and life! O come!
Make once more my heart thy home!

– *Percy Bysshe Shelley*

The Languid Lady

The languid lady next appears in state,
Who was not born to carry her own weight;
She lolls, reels, staggers, till some foreign aid
To her own stature lifts the feeble maid.
Then, if ordained to so severe a doom,
She, by just stages, journeys round the room:
But, knowing her own weakness, she despairs
To scale the Alps — that is, ascend the stairs.
My fan! let others say, who laugh at toil;
Fan! hood! glove! scarf! is her laconic style;
And that is spoke with such a dying fall,
That Betty rather sees, than hears the call:
The motion of her lips, and meaning eye,
Piece out th'idea her faint words deny.
O listen with attention most profound!
Her voice is but the shadow of a sound.
And help! oh help! her spirits are so dead,
One hand scarce lifts the other to her head.
If, there, a stubborn pin it triumphs o'er,
She pants! she sinks away! and is more.

Let the robust and the gigantic carve,
Life is not worth so much, she'd rather starve;
But chew she must herself; ah cruel fate!
That Rosalinda can't by proxy eat.

– *Edward Young*

Comfort

As I mused by the hearthside,
Puss said to me;
'there burns the fire, man,
and here sit we.

Four walls around us
against the cold air;
and the latch drawn close
to the draughty stair.

A roof o'er our heads
star-proof, moon immune,
and a wind in the chimney
to wail us a tune.'

'What felicity!' miaowed he,
'where none may intrude;
just man and beast – met
in this solitude!'

'Dear God, what security,
comfort and bliss!
and to think, too what ages
have brought us to this!'

'You in your sheep's' wool coat,
buttons of bone,
and me in my fur-about
on the warm hearthstone'

– *Walter de la Mare*

To Sleep

O soft embalmer of the still midnight,
Shutting, with careful fingers and benign,
Our gloom-pleased eyes, embowered from the light,
Enshaded in forgetfulness divine:
O soothest Sleep! if so it please thee, close
In midst of this thine hymn my willing eyes,
Or wait the 'Amen,' ere thy poppy throws
Around my bed its lulling charities.
Then save me, or the passed day will shine
Upon my pillow, breeding many woes, –
Save me from curious Conscience, that still lords
Its strength for darkness, burrowing like a mole;
Turn the key deftly in the oiled wards,
And seal the hushed Casket of my Soul.

– John Keats

The Poet's Calendar: October

My ornaments are fruits; my garments leaves,
Woven like cloth of gold, and crimson dyed;
I do not boast the harvesting of sheaves,
O'er orchards and o'er vineyards I preside.
Though on the frigid Scorpion I ride,
The dreamy air is full, and overflows
With tender memories of the summer-tide,
And mingled voices of the doves and crows.

– Henry Wadsworth Longfellow

Fashion

Fair Eve devised a walking-suit
    Of jungle grasses, soft and crimpy;
She thought it rather neat and cute
    Till Adam grunted, 'Pretty skimpy!'

A cloak of palm-leaves, sought for miles,
    She made, and came to be admired;
But Adam said, 'The silly styles
    You women wear just make me tired!'

She built herself a little hat
    Of lilies (Eve was *very* clever),
And asked him what he thought of *that?*
    And Adam blurted, 'Well, I *never!*'

So next she placed upon her head
    A feathered three-by-four Creation. –
The little word that Adam said
    Is barred from parlour conversation.

Yet Eve refused to be a dowd,
    And tied an autumn-tinted sash on.
'I'll dress to please *myself!*' she vowed,
    'For what does Adam know of fashion?

'What use to seek applause from him?
    He scoffs and says I cannot reason!
Well, then, *my* law shall be my whim –
    And that shall change with every season.'

Since when, revolving cycles bring
    The gayest fashions and the queerest;
And Eve declares, 'It's just the thing!'
    And Adam murmurs, 'Is it, dearest?'

– *Arthur Guiterman*

Japanesque

Oh, where the white quince blossom swings
    I love to take my Japan ease!
I love the maid Anise who clings
    So lightly on my Japan knees;
I love the little song she sings,
    The little love-song Japanese.
I *almost* love the lute's *tink-tunkle*
    Played by that charming Jap Anise –
For am I not her old Jap uncle?
    And is she not my Japan niece?

– *Oliver Herford*

An Astrologer's Song

♎

To the Heavens above us
Oh, look and behold
The planets that love us
All harnessed in gold!
What chariots, what horses,
Against us shall bide
While the Stars in their courses
Do fight on our side?

All thought, all desires,
That are under the sun,
Are one with their fires,
As we also are one;
All matter, all spirit,
All fashion, all frame,
Receive and inherit
Their stength from the same.

Earth quakes in her throes
And we wonder for why!
But the blind planet knows

When her ruler is nigh;
And, attuned since Creation,
To perfect accord,
She thrills in her station
And yearns to her Lord.

Then, doubt not, ye fearful –
The Eternal is King –
Up, heart, and be cheerful,
And lustily sing:
What chariots, what horses,
Against us shall bide
While the Stars in their courses
Do fight on our side?

— *Rudyard Kipling*

Not From The Stars . . .

Not from the stars do I my judgment pluck;
And yet methinks I have astronomy,
But not to tell of good or evil luck,
Of plagues, of dearths, or seasons' quality;
Nor can I fortune to brief minutes tell,
Pointing to each his thunder, rain and wind,
Or say with princes if it shall go well,
By oft predict that I in heaven find:
But from thine eyes my knowledge I derive,
And, constant stars, in them I read such art
As truth and beauty shall together thrive,
If from thyself to store thou wouldst convert;
Or else of thee this I prognosticate:
Thy end is truth's and beauty's doom and date.

– *William Shakespeare*

Index

Alcott, Louisa May	Swallow, Swallow	83
Anon	Bobby Shafto	14
	The Lonely Maid	50
Brooke, Rupert	Beauty And Beauty	21
	The Dance	64
Bronte, Emily	Song	84
	The Bluebell	90
Browning, Elizabeth Barrett	How Do I Love Thee?	2
Bryant, William Cullen	October	97
Burgess, Gelett	Ballade Of The Devil-May-Care	27
Bynner, Witter	To Any One	38
Byron, Lord	When We Two Parted	3
	A Long, Long Kiss	47
	She Walks In Beauty	58
	So, We'll Go No More A-Roving	66
	For Music	71
Campion, Thomas	The Measure Of Beauty	20
Clare, John	I Dreamt Of Robin	8
Corbin, Alice	Love Me At Last	86
Cuthbertson, James Lister	Wattle And Myrtle	78
De la Mare, Walter	Comfort	110
Derham, Edith	The Suburbs	77

De Vere, Edward	If Women Could Be Fair And Yet Not Fond	40
Dickinson, Emily	Precious To Me	35
Elizabeth I, Queen	When I Was Fair And Young	67
Donne, John	The Bait	12
	The Anniversary	61
Dowson, Ernest	Ad Manus Puellæ	18
Foster, Stephen	Beautiful Dreamer	24
Gilbert, W. S.	Sad Is That Woman's Lot	88
Goldsmith, Oliver	An Elegy On The Glory Of Her Sex, Mrs Mary Blaize	75
Gordon, Adam Lindsay	September In Australia	94
Guiterman, Arthur	Fashion	114
Hart, Lorenz	Sentimental Me	25
Hartley, Marsden	The Flatterers	100
Herford, Oliver	Japanesque	116
Herrick, Robert	Meditation For His Mistress	52
	Julia's Voice	74
Hood, Thomas	Ruth	56
Keats, John	To Sleep	112
Kemble, Frances Anne	Dream Land	29
Kendall, Henry	A Spanish Love Song	16
Kingsley, Charles	A Myth	98
Kipling, Rudyard	An Astrologer's Song	117
Landor, Walter Savage	No Longer Jealous	30
	Margaret	65
Linton, William James	Love's Blindness	39
Lodge, Thomas	Rosalind's Madrigal	36
Longfellow, Henry Wadsworth	The Poet's Calendar: October	113
Marlowe, Christopher	It Lies Not In Our Power To Love Or Hate	5
	The Passionate Shepherd To His Love	10
Marston, Philip Bourke	Love And Music	80
Pfeiffer, Emily	Love Came Knocking	43

Poe, Edgar Allan	Annabel Lee	31
Radford, Dollie	Spring Song	42
Roscoe, William Caldwell	The Master Chord	72
Rossetti, Christina	Echo	23
	Somewhere Or Other	33
Ruskin, John	Trust Thou Thy Love	34
Shakespeare, William	Cupid Laid By His Brand, And Fell Asleep	15
	Not From The Stars ...	119
Shelley, Percy Bysshe	Love's Philosophy	22
	To Jane, With A Guitar	69
	Music, When Soft Voices Die	73
	Love's Philosophy	97
	Song	105
Stevenson, Robert Louis	Autumn Fires	93
Lord Tennyson, Alfred	Who Is It Comes?	1
Thomson, James	Sunday Up The River	102
Turner, Charles Tennyson	To The Gossamer Light	103
Waller, Edmund	Go, Lovely Rose	59
Watson, William	Estrangement	46
Wilde, Oscar	From Spring Days To Winter	81
	La Fuite De La Lune	104
Yeats, W. B.	A Last Confession	6
	The Cap And Bells	54
	Aedh Gives His Beloved Certain Rhymes	63
Young, Edward	The Languid Lady	108

Derek & Julia Parker

Derek and Julia Parker became internationally famous with the publication of *The Compleat Astrologer* in 1971, the first thorough modern text-book of astrology. A world-wide best-seller, with a new edition released in 1984, it remained in print for twenty years until replaced by *Parkers' Astrology*. Julia Parker remains an active astrologer; Derek (who for five years edited the UK's *Poetry Review*) is also a biographer. They have jointly written books on dream interpretation, popular psychology, travel, the theatre, magic – and love. In 2002, after forty years of working in London, they emigrated to Sydney, where they live with their two wire-haired terriers, Fille and Crim.

Loved the book?

Join thousands of other readers online at

AUSTRALIAN READERS:

randomhouse.com.au/talk

NEW ZEALAND READERS:

randomhouse.co.nz/talk